# JELL-O & CoolWhip
## WHIPPED TOPPING

# Favorite
# Desserts

## pil
Publications
International Ltd.

Favorite Brand Name Recipes at www.fbnr.com

**Pictured on the front cover:** Triple-Layer Lemon Meringue Pie (*page 20*).
**Pictured on the back cover:** Wave-Your-Flag Cheesecake (*page 17*).

**Nutritional Analysis:** Every effort has been made to check the accuracy of the nutritional information that appears with each recipe. However, because numerous variables account for a wide range of values for certain foods, nutritive analyses in this book should be considered approximate. Different results may be obtained by using different nutrient databases and different brand-name products.

**Microwave Cooking:** Microwave ovens vary in wattage. Use the cooking times as guidelines and check for doneness before adding more time.

**Preparation/Cooking Times:** Preparation times are based on the approximate amount of time required to assemble the recipe before cooking, baking, chilling or serving. These times include preparation steps such as measuring, chopping and mixing. The fact that some preparations and cooking can be done simultaneously is taken into account. Preparation of optional ingredients and serving suggestions is not included.

# Contents

22

36

24

8

# Summer Celebrations

Quick, crowd-pleasing summer sweets perfect for picnics, reunions, barbecues, and block parties

## Classic S'mores

Total: 5 minutes

- 4 **JET-PUFFED** Marshmallows, toasted
- 1 milk chocolate candy bar (1.55 ounces), quartered
- 4 **HONEY MAID** Honey Grahams, broken in half (8 squares)

**SANDWICH** 1 toasted marshmallow and 1 chocolate piece between each of 2 graham squares to make each s'more.

*Makes 4 servings, 1 s'more each.*

- - - - - - - - - - - -

*USE YOUR MICROWAVE:* Make indoor s'mores! Top each of 4 graham squares with 1 chocolate piece and 1 untoasted marshmallow. Place on microwaveable plate. Microwave on HIGH 15 to 20 seconds or until marshmallows puff. Top each with a second graham square; press together gently to secure.

# Key Lime Margarita Pie

Total: 6 hours 15 minutes (includes freezing)

1¼ cups crushed pretzels

¼ cup sugar

6 tablespoons butter or margarine, melted

1 can (14 ounces) sweetened condensed milk

½ cup lime juice

1 envelope **KOOL-AID** Lemon Lime Unsweetened Soft Drink Mix

1 tub (8 ounces) **COOL WHIP** Whipped Topping, thawed, divided

MIX crushed pretzels, sugar and butter. Press firmly onto bottom and up side of 9-inch pie plate. Refrigerate until ready to fill.

COMBINE condensed milk, lime juice and drink mix in large bowl until well blended. Remove ½ cup whipped topping; refrigerate until ready to use. Gently stir in remaining whipped topping. Pour into crust.

FREEZE 6 hours or overnight. Let stand at room temperature 15 minutes or until pie can be cut easily. Garnish with reserved whipped topping before serving. Store leftover pie in freezer.

*Makes 10 servings.*

- - - - - - - - -

*JAZZ IT UP:* For added lime flavor, stir in 2 tablespoons grated lime peel with lime juice.

# Peach & Raspberry Trifle

Total: 2 hours 25 minutes (includes refrigerating)

- 3 tablespoons orange juice
- ¼ teaspoon almond extract
- 1 package (9 ounces) prepared angel food cake, cut into 1-inch cubes
- 1 pound ripe peaches, peeled, divided
- ¼ cup raspberry fruit spread
- 2 cups raspberries, divided
- 2¾ cups fat free milk
- 2 packages (4-serving size each) **JELL-O** Vanilla Flavor Fat Free Sugar Free Instant Reduced Calorie Pudding & Pie Filling
- 1½ cups thawed **COOL WHIP LITE** Whipped Topping, divided

**COMBINE** orange juice and almond extract. Drizzle over cake cubes in large bowl; toss lightly. Set aside. Slice peaches; set aside. Mix fruit spread with 1 cup of the raspberries.

**POUR** milk into separate large bowl. Add dry pudding mixes. Beat with wire whisk 2 minutes or until well blended. Gently stir in 1 cup of the whipped topping.

**PLACE** half of the cake cubes in 2-quart glass serving bowl or round baking dish. Top with layers of half each of the raspberries, peaches and pudding mixture. Top with remaining cake cubes, remaining raspberries, peaches and remaining pudding mixture; cover with plastic wrap. Refrigerate at least 2 hours. Top with remaining ½ cup whipped topping just before serving. Store leftover dessert in refrigerator.

*Makes 16 servings, ½ cup each.*

- - - - - - - - - -

*MAKE AHEAD:* Trifle can be made up to 6 hours in advance.

# Citrus Sorbet Pie

Total: 4 hours 20 minutes (includes freezing)

⅔ cup boiling water

1 package (4-serving size) **JELL-O** Orange Flavor Gelatin

1 cup orange sherbet

2 cups thawed **COOL WHIP** Whipped Topping

2 cups **JET-PUFFED** Miniature Marshmallows

1 can (8 ounces) crushed pineapple, drained

1 **HONEY MAID** Graham Pie Crust (6 ounces)

**STIR** boiling water into dry gelatin mix in large bowl at least 2 minutes until completely dissolved. Add sherbet; stir until sherbet is completely melted and mixture is slightly thickened. Add whipped topping, marshmallows and pineapple; stir gently with wire whisk until well blended. Refrigerate 10 minutes or until mixture is very thick and will mound.

**POUR** into crust.

**FREEZE** 4 hours or until firm. Store leftover pie in freezer.

*Makes 8 servings.*

- - - - - - - - - -

*VARIATION:* Prepare as directed, using JELL-O Lime Flavor Gelatin and lemon sherbet.

## 30 Minute Prep — Easy Chocolate Éclair Squares

Total: 3 hours 30 minutes (includes refrigerating)

1¾  cups cold milk

1  package (4-serving size) **JELL-O** Vanilla Flavor Instant Pudding & Pie Filling

1  tub (8 ounces) **COOL WHIP** Whipped Topping, thawed

22  **HONEY MAID** Honey Grahams

3  tablespoons butter or margarine

2  squares **BAKER'S** Unsweetened Baking Chocolate

2  tablespoons cold milk

1  cup sifted powdered sugar

POUR 1¾ cups milk into large bowl. Add dry pudding mix. Beat with wire whisk 2 minutes. Gently stir in whipped topping. Layer one-third of the grahams and half of the whipped topping mixture in 13×9-inch baking pan, breaking grahams as necessary to fit; repeat layers. Top with remaining grahams.

PLACE butter, chocolate and 2 tablespoons milk in small saucepan; cook on low heat until chocolate is completely melted and mixture is blended. Gradually add sugar, stirring until well blended. Spread over grahams.

REFRIGERATE several hours or overnight. Store any leftover dessert in refrigerator.

*Makes 24 servings.*

*"Tastes like an éclair, but oh so easy to make!"*
—*Sarah Dicello, Kraft Kitchens*

# (15 Minute Prep) Lemon-Lime Daiquiri Layered Dessert

Total: 3 hours 25 minutes (includes refrigerating)

- 2 cups lime sherbet, softened
- 1 container (8 ounces) **PHILADELPHIA** Cream Cheese Spread
- 1 can (14 ounces) sweetened condensed milk
- ½ cup lemon juice
- 1 tub (8 ounces) **COOL WHIP** Whipped Topping, thawed

LINE 9×5-inch loaf pan with foil. Spoon sherbet into prepared pan; spread to form even layer in pan. Freeze 10 minutes.

BEAT cream cheese spread in large bowl with wire whisk until creamy. Gradually add sweetened condensed milk and lemon juice, beating until well blended. Stir in whipped topping; spread over sherbet layer in pan.

FREEZE at least 3 hours or overnight. Invert loaf onto a serving plate and remove foil. Garnish with lemon and lime slices, if desired. Cut into 12 slices to serve. Store leftover dessert in freezer.

*Makes 12 servings.*

# Wave-Your-Flag Cake

Total: 20 minutes (includes refrigerating)

| | |
|---|---|
| 1 | quart strawberries (4 cups), divided |
| 1½ | cups boiling water |
| 1 | package (8-serving size) or 2 packages (4-serving size each) **JELL-O** Strawberry Flavor Gelatin |
| | Ice cubes |
| 1 | cup cold water |
| 1 | package (12 ounces) pound cake, cut into 10 slices |
| 1⅓ | cups blueberries, divided |
| 1 | tub (8 ounces) **COOL WHIP** Whipped Topping, thawed |

SLICE 1 cup of the strawberries. Halve remaining strawberries; set aside.

STIR boiling water into dry gelatin mix in large bowl 2 minutes until completely dissolved. Add enough ice to cold water to measure 2 cups. Add to gelatin; stir until ice is melted. Refrigerate 5 minutes or until slightly thickened (consistency of unbeaten egg whites). Meanwhile, line bottom of 13×9-inch dish with cake slices. Add sliced strawberries and 1 cup of the blueberries to thickened gelatin; stir gently. Spoon over cake slices.

REFRIGERATE 4 hours or until firm. Spread whipped topping over gelatin. Arrange strawberry halves on whipped topping for "stripes" of "flag." Arrange remaining ⅓ cup blueberries on whipped topping for "stars." Store in refrigerator.

*Makes 18 servings.*

- - - - - - - - - -

*WAVE-YOUR-FLAG CHEESECAKE:* Prepare cake and gelatin layers as directed. Refrigerate 4 hours or until firm. Beat 2 packages (8 ounces each) softened PHILADELPHIA Cream Cheese and ¼ cup sugar with wire whisk or electric mixer until well blended; gently stir in whipped topping. Spread over gelatin layer. Continue as directed.

# JELL-O Mini Trifle Bites

Total: 2 hours 10 minutes (includes refrigerating)

2   cups boiling water

2   packages (4-serving size each) **JELL-O** Raspberry Flavor
    Sugar Free Low Calorie Gelatin

3   slices (¾-inch-thick each) fat free pound cake, cut into 24 cubes

1   package (8 ounces) **PHILADELPHIA** Neufchâtel Cheese,
    ⅓ Less Fat than Cream Cheese, softened

1   cup powdered sugar

1   cup thawed **COOL WHIP LITE** Whipped Topping

1   teaspoon grated lemon peel

PLACE foil liners in 24 miniature muffin pan cups. Stir boiling water
into dry gelatin mixes in large bowl 2 minutes until completely
dissolved. Place 1 cake cube in each muffin cup; pour gelatin over
cake to fill cup completely. Refrigerate 2 hours or until set.

BEAT cream cheese in small bowl with electric mixer on medium
speed until creamy. Gradually add sugar, beating until well blended
after each addition. Gently stir in whipped topping and lemon peel
until well blended.

FILL pastry bag fitted with star tip with cream cheese mixture. Pipe
decorative dollop of cream cheese mixture on top of each trifle.

*Makes 12 servings, 2 trifles each.*

- - - - - - - - - -

*SUBSTITUTE:* This recipe can be made with any flavor JELL-O Gelatin.

# Triple-Layer Lemon Meringue Pie

**(15 Minute Prep)**

Total: 3 hours 15 minutes (includes refrigerating)

- 2 cups cold milk
- 2 packages (4-serving size each) **JELL-O** Lemon Flavor Instant Pudding & Pie Filling
- 1 tablespoon lemon juice
- 1 **HONEY MAID** Graham Pie Crust (6 ounces)
- 1 tub (8 ounces) **COOL WHIP** Whipped Topping, thawed, divided
- 2½ cups **JET-PUFFED** Miniature Marshmallows, divided
- 2 tablespoons cold milk

**POUR** 2 cups milk into large bowl. Add dry pudding mixes and juice. Beat with wire whisk 2 minutes or until well blended. (Mixture will be thick.)

**SPREAD** 1½ cups of the pudding onto bottom of crust; set aside. Add half of the whipped topping to remaining pudding; stir gently until well blended. Spread over pudding layer in crust. Place 2 cups of the marshmallows in large microwaveable bowl. Add 2 tablespoons milk; stir. Microwave on HIGH 1½ minutes or until marshmallows are completely melted, stirring after 1 minute. Stir until well blended. Refrigerate 15 minutes or until cooled. Gently stir in whipped topping; spread over pudding mixture.

**REFRIGERATE** 3 hours or until set. Top with the remaining ½ cup marshmallows just before serving. Store leftover pie in refrigerator.

*Makes 8 servings, 1 slice each.*

- - - - - - - - - -

*JAZZ IT UP*: Garnish with lemon twists or ½ cup sliced strawberries just before serving.

"Marshmallows are the secret ingredient
in this easy, impressive meringue."
—Sarah Dicello, Kraft Kitchens

# Melon Bubbles

Total: 4 hours 45 minutes (includes refrigerating)

1½   cups boiling water

2   packages (4-serving size each) **JELL-O** Melon Fusion Gelatin

2½   cups cold club soda

⅓   cup each: cantaloupe, honeydew and watermelon balls

STIR boiling water into dry gelatin mix in large bowl at least 2 minutes until completely dissolved. Stir in club soda. Refrigerate 1½ hours or until thickened (spoon drawn through leaves definite impression).

MEASURE 1 cup thickened gelatin into medium bowl; set aside. Stir melon balls into remaining gelatin. Spoon into 8 dessert glasses.

BEAT reserved gelatin with electric mixer on high speed until fluffy and about doubled in volume. Spoon over gelatin in glasses. Refrigerate 3 hours or until firm. Store any leftover desserts in refrigerator.

*Makes 8 servings.*

- - - - - - - -

*SUBSTITUTE:* Prepare as directed, using seltzer instead of club soda.

# Cool 'n Icy Treats

## Fantastic frosty desserts and beverages

### OREO Ice Cream Shop Pie

Total: 4 hours 15 minutes (includes freezing)

| | |
|---|---|
| ½ | cup hot fudge dessert topping, divided |
| 1 | **OREO** Pie Crust (6 ounces) |
| 1 | tub (8 ounces) **COOL WHIP** Whipped Topping, thawed, divided |
| 1¼ | cups cold milk |
| 2 | packages (4-serving size each) **JELL-O OREO** Flavor Instant Pudding & Pie Filling |

REMOVE 2 tablespoons of the fudge topping; refrigerate for later use. Spoon remaining topping into crust; spread to evenly cover bottom of crust. Top with half of the whipped topping; freeze 10 minutes.

POUR milk into large bowl. Add dry pudding mixes. Beat with wire whisk 2 minutes or until well blended. (Mixture will be thick.) Gently stir in remaining whipped topping. Spoon over whipped topping layer in crust.

FREEZE 4 hours or until firm. Remove pie from freezer 15 minutes before serving. Let stand at room temperature to soften slightly. Drizzle with the reserved 2 tablespoons fudge topping. Store leftover pie in freezer.

*Makes 10 servings.*

- - - - - - - - - - - - -

*SUBSTITUTE:* Prepare as directed using a HONEY MAID Pie Crust.

# Frozen Lemonade Squares

Total: 4 hours 20 minutes (includes freezing)

9    **HONEY MAID** Low Fat Honey Grahams, finely crushed (about 1 ¼ cups crumbs)

⅓    cup margarine or butter, melted

1    quart (4 cups) frozen vanilla yogurt, softened

1    can (6 ounces) frozen lemonade concentrate, thawed

½    cup thawed **COOL WHIP LITE** Whipped Topping

Fresh mint sprigs and lemon slices (optional)

MIX graham crumbs and margarine. Press firmly onto bottom of 9-inch square pan.

BEAT yogurt and lemonade concentrate in large bowl with electric mixer on medium speed until well blended. Spread over crust.

FREEZE 4 hours or until firm. Cut into squares. Top each square with a dollop of whipped topping. Garnish with fresh mint sprigs and lemon slices, if desired.

*Makes 9 servings, 1 square each.*

- - - - - - - - -

*JAZZ IT UP:* Serve this refreshing dessert with fresh raspberries.

## Frosty Orange Dream Squares

*20 Minute Prep*

Total: 3 hours 20 minutes (includes freezing)

40 **NILLA** Wafers, finely crushed (about 1½ cups)

¼ cup (½ stick) butter, melted

2 cups cold milk

2 packages (4-serving size each) **JELL-O** Vanilla Flavor Instant Pudding & Pie Filling

1 tub (8 ounces) **COOL WHIP** Whipped Topping, thawed, divided

1 pint (2 cups) orange sherbet, softened

LINE 13×9-inch pan with foil, with ends of foil extending over sides of pan. Combine wafer crumbs and butter. Press firmly onto bottom of prepared pan; set aside until ready to use.

ADD milk to dry pudding mixes in medium bowl. Beat with wire whisk 2 minutes or until well blended. Gently stir in half of the whipped topping. Spoon evenly over crust. Refrigerate 10 minutes. Add remaining whipped topping to sherbet; stir with wire whisk until well blended. Spoon evenly over pudding layer; cover.

FREEZE at least 3 hours or overnight. Use foil handles to remove dessert from pan before cutting into squares to serve. Store leftover dessert in freezer.

*Makes 24 servings, 1 square each.*

- - - - - - - - - -

*SUBSTITUTE:* Prepare as directed, using lime or raspberry sherbet.

"This classic flavor combo is sure to bring back memories of a favorite summer dessert."
—Sarah Dicello, Kraft Kitchens

# No-Melt Sundae Pie

Total: 6 hours 15 minutes (includes refrigerating)

15 **OREO** Chocolate Sandwich Cookies, crushed (about 1½ cups crumbs)

3 tablespoons butter, melted

1 tub (8 ounces) **COOL WHIP** Whipped Topping, thawed, divided

1 cup cold milk

1 package (4-serving size) **JELL-O** Vanilla Flavor Instant Pudding & Pie Filling

2 squares **BAKER'S** Semi-Sweet Baking Chocolate, melted

⅓ cup canned sweetened condensed milk

MIX crumbs and butter; press onto bottom and up side of 9-inch pie plate. Reserve ½ cup of the whipped topping. Refrigerate until ready to use.

POUR milk into large bowl. Add dry pudding mix. Beat with wire whisk 2 minutes or until well blended. Gently stir in remaining whipped topping. Spoon into crust. Mix melted chocolate and condensed milk until well blended. Spoon over pie. Cut through chocolate mixture several times with knife for marble effect.

FREEZE 6 hours or until firm. Remove pie from freezer 15 minutes before serving. Let stand at room temperature to soften slightly. Top with the reserved whipped topping.

*Makes 10 servings.*

# Frozen Chocolate Soufflés

Total: 5 hours 10 minutes (includes freezing)

3 cups cold milk

1 package (8-serving size) or 2 packages (4-serving size each) **JELL-O** Chocolate Flavor Instant Pudding & Pie Filling

2 cups thawed **COOL WHIP** Whipped Topping

16 **OREO** Chocolate Sandwich Cookies, chopped (about 2 cups)

8 maraschino cherries

POUR milk into medium bowl. Add dry pudding mix. Beat with wire whisk 2 minutes. Gently stir in whipped topping.

SPOON 2 tablespoons of the chopped cookies into each of 8 (8- to 9-ounce) paper drinking cups. Cover evenly with half of the pudding mixture. Repeat layers. Cover with foil.

FREEZE 5 hours or until firm. Remove from freezer about 15 minutes before serving. Let stand at room temperature to soften slightly. Peel away paper to unmold soufflés onto plates. Top each with a cherry. Store leftover soufflés in freezer.

*Makes 8 servings, 1 soufflé each.*

- - - - - - - - - -

*VARIATION:* Prepare as directed, using JELL-O Vanilla Flavor Instant Pudding & Pie Filling and CHIPS AHOY! Real Chocolate Chip Cookies.

# OREO & Fudge Ice Cream Cake

Total: 4 hours 10 minutes (includes freezing)

½ cup hot fudge dessert topping, warmed

1 tub (8 ounces) **COOL WHIP** Whipped Topping, thawed, divided

1 package (4-serving size) **JELL-O** Chocolate Flavor Instant Pudding & Pie Filling

8 **OREO** Chocolate Sandwich Cookies, chopped (about 1 cup)

12 vanilla ice cream sandwiches

POUR fudge topping into medium bowl. Add 1 cup of the whipped topping; stir with wire whisk until well blended. Add dry pudding mix; stir 2 minutes or until well blended. Gently stir in chopped cookies; set aside.

ARRANGE 4 of the ice cream sandwiches, side-by-side, on 24-inch-long piece of foil; top with half of the whipped topping mixture. Repeat layers. Top with remaining 4 ice cream sandwiches. Frost top and sides of dessert with remaining whipped topping. Bring up foil sides. Double fold top and ends to loosely seal packet.

FREEZE at least 4 hours before serving. Store leftover dessert in freezer.

*Makes 12 servings.*

- - - - - - - - - -

*SUBSTITUTE:* Prepare as directed, using Neapolitan ice cream sandwiches.

*"Great for entertaining because it's deliciously easy to make ahead."*
—*Sarah Dicello, Kraft Kitchens*

# "Sangria" Fruit Cups

Total: 4 hours 20 minutes (includes refrigerating)

   1   cup orange juice
   1   package (4-serving size) **JELL-O** Strawberry Flavor Gelatin
   1   package (4-serving size) **JELL-O** Lemon Flavor Gelatin
1½   cups cold water
   1   cup pitted fresh sweet cherries, halved
   1   cup quartered strawberries (about 8 medium)
   1   cup sliced peeled nectarines (about 1 medium)
   1   cup thawed **COOL WHIP** Whipped Topping

BRING orange juice to boil. Add to dry gelatin mixes in medium bowl; stir at least 2 minutes until gelatin is completely dissolved. Stir in cold water.

SPOON fruit evenly into 8 clear cups. Pour gelatin mixture over fruit.

REFRIGERATE 4 hours or until firm. Top with whipped topping just before serving. Store leftover desserts in refrigerator.

*Makes 8 servings, about ½ cup each.*

- - - - - - - - - -

*SUBSTITUTE:* Substitute seedless grape halves for the cherries.

# Creamy Carnival Cups

Total: 40 minutes (includes refrigerating)

1 cup boiling water

1 package (4-serving size) **JELL-O** Strawberry Flavor Gelatin

2 cups vanilla ice cream

⅓ cup thawed **COOL WHIP** Whipped Topping

STIR boiling water into dry gelatin mix in medium bowl at least 2 minutes until completely dissolved. Stir in ice cream with wire whisk until well blended.

POUR into 6 dessert bowls. Refrigerate 30 minutes or until set.

TOP each serving with about 1 tablespoon whipped topping just before serving.

*Makes 6 servings, ½ cup each.*

- - - - - - - - - -

*SUBSTITUTE:* Prepare as directed, using JELL-O Lemon Flavor Gelatin.

# Frozen Peach Shortcake Squares

### 10 Minute Prep

Total: 3 hours 10 minutes (includes refrigerating)

- 1 tub (8 ounces) **COOL WHIP** Whipped Topping, thawed
- 1 pint (2 cups) vanilla ice cream, softened
- 1 package (4-serving size) **JELL-O** Peach Flavor Gelatin
- 4 cups pound cake cubes
- ¼ cup raspberry preserves
- 12 small peach slices
- 12 raspberries

MIX whipped topping, ice cream and dry gelatin mix in large bowl until well blended. Stir in cake cubes. Spoon into 8-inch square pan.

FREEZE 3 hours or until firm.

DRIZZLE with raspberry preserves. Cut into squares. Top each square with 1 peach slice and 1 raspberry. Store any leftover dessert in freezer.

*Makes 12 servings, 1 square each.*

# Frosty Lemon Ice

Total: 3 hours 20 minutes (includes refrigerating)

1 cup boiling water

1 package (4-serving size) **JELL-O** Lemon Flavor Sugar Free Low Calorie Gelatin

1 cup chilled lemon lime-flavored seltzer

½ teaspoon grated lemon peel

3 tablespoons fresh lemon juice

STIR boiling water into dry gelatin mix in medium bowl at least 2 minutes until completely dissolved. Stir in seltzer, lemon peel and juice. Pour into 9-inch square pan; cover.

FREEZE 3 hours or until frozen. Let stand at room temperature 10 minutes.

BEAT with electric mixer or blend in covered blender container on high speed until smooth. Spoon into dessert dishes. Store leftover ice in freezer.

*Makes 6 servings.*

- - - - - - - - - -

*JAZZ IT UP:* Garnish with fresh lemon slices and mint sprigs.

# Rocket Pops

Total: 7 hours 30 minutes (includes refrigerating)

- 1 package (4-serving size) **JELL-O** Cherry Flavor Gelatin
- 1 cup sugar, divided
- 2 cups boiling water, divided
  Ice cubes
- 2 cups cold water, divided
- 1 package (4-serving size) **JELL-O** Berry Blue Flavor Gelatin
- 1 tub (8 ounces) **COOL WHIP** Whipped Topping, thawed

COMBINE dry cherry gelatin mix and ½ cup of the sugar in medium bowl. Add 1 cup of the boiling water; stir at least 2 minutes until gelatin is completely dissolved. Add enough ice cubes to 1 cup of the cold water to measure 2 cups. Add to gelatin; stir until ice is completely melted. Pour evenly into 16 (5-ounce) paper or plastic cups, adding about ¼ cup of the gelatin to each cup. Freeze 1 hour.

MEANWHILE, combine dry blue gelatin mix and remaining ½ cup sugar in medium bowl. Add remaining 1 cup boiling water; stir at least 2 minutes until gelatin is completely dissolved. Add enough ice cubes to remaining 1 cup cold water to measure 2 cups. Add to gelatin; stir until ice is completely melted. Refrigerate 1 hour.

SPOON about 3 tablespoons of the whipped topping over red gelatin in each cup; top evenly with blue gelatin, adding about ¼ cup of the gelatin to each cup. Freeze 1 hour or until almost firm. Insert wooden pop stick or plastic spoon into center of each cup for handle. Freeze an additional 4 hours or overnight. To remove pops from cups, place bottoms of cups under warm running water for 15 seconds. Press firmly on bottoms of cups to release pops. (Do not twist or pull pop sticks.) Store leftover pops in freezer.

*Makes 16 servings.*

# Mixed Berry Smoothie

Total: 10 minutes

2   cups cold milk

1   container (6 ounces) strawberry low-fat yogurt

1   package (4-serving size) **JELL-O** Strawberry Flavor Gelatin

1   cup frozen mixed berries

2   biscuits **POST** Shredded Wheat Cereal, crumbled

PLACE all ingredients in blender; cover.

BLEND on high speed 15 seconds or until smooth.

SERVE immediately.

*Makes 4 servings, about 1 cup each.*

- - - - - - - - - -

*FRESH BANANA PUDDING SMOOTHIE:* Prepare as directed, using 3 cups milk, 1 package (4-serving size) JELL-O Vanilla Flavor Instant Pudding and Pie Filling, 2 ripe bananas and ½ cup POST SELECTS BANANA NUT CRUNCH Cereal.

*PEACHY STRAWBERRY SMOOTHIE:* Prepare as directed, using 1½ cups milk, 1 container (6 ounces) plain nonfat yogurt, 1½ teaspoons CRYSTAL LIGHT Raspberry Ice Flavor Low Calorie Soft Drink Mix, 1 cup each frozen sliced peaches and frozen strawberries and ½ cup POST HONEY BUNCHES OF OATS Cereal.

# Frozen Coolwich

Total: 4 hours 15 minutes (includes refrigerating)

½  cup hot fudge dessert topping

10  **HONEY MAID** Honey Grahams, broken in half (20 squares)

2  cups thawed **COOL WHIP** Whipped Topping

¼  cup multi-colored sprinkles

SPREAD hot fudge topping evenly onto 10 of the graham squares.

COVER each of the 10 remaining graham squares with about a ¾-inch-thick layer of whipped topping; top each with a fudge-topped square, fudge side down, to make sandwich. Press together lightly to secure. Roll or lightly press edges in sprinkles.

FREEZE 4 hours or overnight. Wrap individually with plastic wrap or foil. Store in freezer up to 2 weeks.

*Makes 10 servings.*

- - - - - - - - -

*SUBSTITUTE:* Any number of garnishes can be used in place of the sprinkles, including small candies, finely crushed NABISCO Cookies, chopped candy bars and toasted BAKER'S ANGEL FLAKE Coconut.

# Berry-licious Delights

Delcious desserts using summer fruits

 ## Summer Berry Pie

Total: 4 hours 30 minutes (includes refrigerating)

- ¾ cup sugar
- 3 tablespoons cornstarch
- 1½ cups water
- 1 package (4-serving size) **JELL-O** Strawberry Flavor Gelatin
- 1 cup each: blueberries, raspberries and sliced strawberries
- 1 **HONEY MAID** Graham Pie Crust (6 ounces)
- 1½ cups thawed **COOL WHIP** Whipped Topping

**MIX** sugar and cornstarch in medium saucepan. Gradually add water, stirring until well blended. Bring to boil on medium heat, stirring constantly; boil 1 minute. Remove from heat. Add dry gelatin mix; stir until dissolved. Stir in fruit.

**POUR** into crust.

**REFRIGERATE** 3 hours or until firm. Top with whipped topping just before serving. Store any leftover pie in refrigerator.

*Makes 10 servings.*

# Fast Fruity Delight

Take ¾ cup boiling water and 1 cup thawed **COOL WHIP** Whipped Topping and mix & match your recipe from these options...

| **JELL-O** Gelatin Flavor options | **frozen fruit** choices |
|---|---|
| Strawberry | strawberries |
| Blackberry Fusion (featured in photo) | raspberries |
| Orange | mixed fruit blend |
| Berry Blue | blueberries |

Just follow our 3 simple steps:

1. Stir boiling water into 1 package (4-serving size) **JELL-O Gelatin** in large bowl at least 2 minutes until completely dissolved.

2. Add 2 cups **frozen fruit**; stir until gelatin starts to thicken. Mix ½ cup of the gelatin mixture into whipped topping with wire whisk until well blended.

3. Spoon whipped topping mixture evenly into 4 dessert cups. Spoon remaining gelatin and fruit mixture over whipped topping mixture in each cup. Refrigerate 15 minutes or until set. Store any leftover dessert cups in refrigerator.

*Makes 4 servings.*

- - - - - - - - -

*MAKE IT EASY:* The frozen fruit makes setting the gelatin quick and easy.

## (10 Minute Prep) Berry Crunch Parfait

Total: 10 minutes

½   cup sliced strawberries

2   tablespoons thawed **COOL WHIP LITE** Whipped Topping

2   tablespoons **POST HONEY BUNCHES OF OATS** Cereal

**PLACE** half of the strawberries in 8-ounce glass; top with layers of 1 tablespoon each of the whipped topping and cereal.

**COVER** with layers of the remaining strawberries and cereal.

**TOP** with the remaining whipped topping.

*Makes 1 serving.*

- - - - - - - - -

*SUBSTITUTE:* Prepare as directed, substituting your favorite summer berries for the sliced strawberries.

# Mixed Berry Freezer Jam

Total 30 minutes plus standing

1 quart strawberries, stemmed, mashed

1 pint raspberries, mashed

1 pint blueberries, mashed

3 cups sugar

1 box **SURE-JELL** For Less or No Sugar Needed Recipes Premium Fruit Pectin

1 cup water

**MEASURE** 2 cups mashed strawberries and 1 cup each mashed raspberries and blueberries into large bowl; mix well.

**BRING** sugar, pectin and water to a boil in large saucepan, stirring constantly. Boil and stir 1 minute. Remove from heat.

**ADD** fruit mixture; stir 1 minute or until thoroughly mixed.

**FILL** clean plastic containers immediately to within ½-inch of tops; cover with lids. Let stand at room temperature for 24 hours until set. Store in refrigerator up to 3 weeks or freeze extra containers up to 1 year. Thaw in refrigerator before using.

*Makes about 7 (1-cup) containers, or 112 servings, 1 tablespoon each.*

– – – – – – – – – –

*NOTE:* This jam is the essence of summer. It's so good, you'll want to keep some in the freezer for year-round enjoyment.

**15 Minute Prep**

# PHILADELPHIA "Fruit Smoothie" No-Bake Cheesecake

Total: 4 hours 15 minutes (includes refrigerating)

- 1½ cups **HONEY MAID** Graham Cracker Crumbs
- ¼ cup (½ stick) butter, melted
- 2 tablespoons sugar
- 4 packages (8 ounces each) **PHILADELPHIA** Neufchâtel Cheese, ⅓ Less Fat than Cream Cheese, softened
- ½ cup sugar
- 1 package (12 ounces) frozen mixed berries (strawberries, raspberries, blueberries and blackberries), thawed, drained
- 1 tub (8 ounces) **COOL WHIP LITE** Whipped Topping, thawed

**LINE** 13×9-inch baking pan with foil, with ends of foil extending over sides of pan. Mix graham crumbs, butter and 2 tablespoons sugar; press firmly onto bottom of prepared pan. Refrigerate while preparing filling.

**BEAT** Neufchâtel cheese and ½ cup sugar in large bowl with electric mixer on medium speed until well blended. Smash drained berries with fork; stir into Neufchâtel cheese mixture. Gently stir in whipped topping. Spoon over crust; cover.

**REFRIGERATE** 4 hours or until firm. Use foil handles to remove cheesecake from pan before cutting into pieces to serve. Store leftover cheesecake in refrigerator.

*Makes 16 servings, 1 piece each.*

- - - - - - - - - -

*SUBSTITUTE:* Prepare as directed, substituting 3 cups fresh mixed berries for the 12-ounce package of frozen mixed berries and increasing the sugar in the Neufchâtel cheese mixture from ½ cup to ¾ cup.

# Cherry Celebration

Total 4 hours 30 minutes

2   cups boiling water

2   packages (4-serving size each) **JELL-O** Cherry Flavor Gelatin

4   cups ice cubes

3   cups thawed **COOL WHIP** Whipped Topping

1   cup cherry pie filling

**STIR** boiling water into dry gelatin mix in large bowl until completely dissolved. Add ice cubes; stir until gelatin begins to thicken. Remove any unmelted ice.

**ADD** whipped topping; stir with wire whisk until well blended. Refrigerate until slightly thickened, about 20 minutes.

**ADD** cherry pie filling; stir gently until well blended. Spoon into 12 champagne glasses or a glass bowl. Refrigerate 4 hours or overnight. Garnish with additional whipped topping and cherry pie filling just before serving, if desired.

*Makes 12 servings, ⅔ cup each.*

- - - - - - - - - -

*JAZZ IT UP:* For an extra special touch, use a spoon to drizzle melted BAKER'S Baking Chocolate on inside of empty serving bowl. Refrigerate several hours or overnight. Fill with pie filling mixture and refrigerate as directed.

# Berry Squares

Total: 1 hour 15 minutes (includes refrigerating)

1 package (12 ounces) pound cake, cut into 10 slices

3 tablespoons orange juice

2 pints fresh berries (strawberries, raspberries and/or blueberries)

2 tablespoons sugar

2½ cups cold milk

2 packages (4-serving size each) **JELL-O** French Vanilla Flavor Instant Pudding & Pie Filling

1 tub (8 ounces) **COOL WHIP** Whipped Topping, thawed, divided

**ARRANGE** cake slices on bottom of 13×9-inch dish, cutting to fit if necessary; drizzle with juice. Top with berries; sprinkle with sugar.

**POUR** milk into large bowl. Add dry pudding mixes. Beat with wire whisk 2 minutes. Gently stir in 1 cup of the whipped topping; spread over berries. Top with remaining whipped topping.

**REFRIGERATE** at least 1 hour before cutting into squares to serve.

*Makes 15 servings, 1 square each.*

---------

*HEALTHY LIVING:* For a low-fat version of this luscious dessert, prepare with fat free pound cake, fat free milk, JELL-O Vanilla Flavor Fat Free Sugar Free Instant Reduced Calorie Pudding & Pie Filling and COOL WHIP FREE Whipped Topping. It has 80 fewer calories and 80% less fat per serving.

# JELL-O Magic Mousse

Total: 8 hours 10 minutes (includes refrigerating)

1 ½   cups boiling water

1   package (4-serving size) **JELL-O** Strawberry Flavor Gelatin

1   tub (8 ounces **COOL WHIP** Whipped Topping, thawed

1   cup fresh berries (sliced strawberries, blueberries and raspberries)

**STIR** boiling water into dry gelatin mix in medium bowl at least 2 minutes until completely dissolved. Add whipped topping; stir with wire whisk until whipped topping is completely melted and mixture is well blended. (Mixture will be thin.)

**FILL** dessert cups evenly with gelatin mixture.

**REFRIGERATE** at least 2 hours or until layers separate. Top with fruit. Store leftover desserts in refrigerator.

*Makes 5 servings, about ½ cup each.*

- - - - - - - - - -

*SHORTCUT:* Is the whipped topping still frozen? No need to worry. Just follow the recipe as directed, using the still-frozen whipped topping. Just be sure to stir the gelatin mixture until the whipped topping is completely melted as directed before pouring into the prepared mold.

*"The frozen whipped topping melts into the gelatin causing it to magically separate into two layers."*
—*Sarah Dicello, Kraft Kitchens*

## (10 Minute Prep) Sparkling Berry Dessert

Total: 4 hours 40 minutes (includes refrigerating)

1½  cups boiling water

1  package (8-serving size) **JELL-O** Raspberry Flavor Gelatin

2½  cups cold club soda

1  cup sliced strawberries

**STIR** boiling water into dry gelatin mix in large bowl at least 2 minutes until completely dissolved. Add club soda; stir. Refrigerate 1½ hours or until thickened (spoon drawn through leaves definite impression).

**REMOVE** 1 cup of the thickened gelatin; place in medium bowl. Set aside. Stir strawberries into remaining gelatin. Spoon evenly into 8 champagne glasses or dessert dishes.

**BEAT** reserved 1 cup gelatin with electric mixer on high speed until fluffy and about doubled in volume. Spoon over gelatin in glasses; cover. Refrigerate 3 hours or until firm. Store any leftover desserts in refrigerator.

*Makes 8 servings.*

----------

*SUBSTITUTE:* Prepare as directed, using seltzer instead of club soda.

# Triple Berry Parfaits

Total: 15 minutes

⅔ cup each: raspberries, sliced strawberries and blueberries

3 containers (6 ounces each) strawberry nonfat yogurt

¼ cup **BAKER'S ANGEL FLAKE** Coconut

24 Reduced Fat **NILLA** Wafers, coarsely chopped

6 tablespoons thawed **COOL WHIP LITE** Whipped Topping

**MIX** fruit in medium bowl. Add yogurt and coconut; toss to coat.

**SPOON** half of the chopped wafers evenly into 6 parfait glasses; cover with half of the fruit mixture. Repeat layers.

**TOP** with the whipped topping.

*Makes 6 servings.*

- - - - - - - - -

*MAKE AHEAD:* Prepare parfaits as directed. Cover and refrigerate up to 1 hour before serving.

# Strawberry Dessert Pizza

Total: 40 minutes

1   package (20 ounces) refrigerated sugar cookie dough

1   package (8 ounces) **PHILADELPHIA** Cream Cheese, softened

⅓   cup sugar

1   tub (8 ounces) **COOL WHIP** Strawberry Whipped Topping, thawed

1   pint (2 cups) strawberries, sliced

**PREHEAT** oven to 350°F. Press dough firmly into greased 12-inch pizza pan. Bake 20 minutes or until golden brown. Cool in pan on wire rack.

**BEAT** cream cheese and sugar in large bowl with wire whisk or electric mixer on high speed until well blended. Gently stir in whipped topping.

**SPREAD** cream cheese mixture over crust; top with strawberries. Serve immediately. Or cover and refrigerate until ready to serve. Store any leftover dessert in refrigerator.

*Makes 12 servings.*

- - - - - - - - -

*SUBSTITUTE:* Prepare as directed, using regular COOL WHIP Whipped Topping.

*"Easy as pie to make! I also like using raspberries and blueberries with the strawberries."*
*—Sarah Dicello, Kraft Kitchens*

# SURE-JELL Strawberry Jam

Total: 45 minutes

5   cups prepared fruit (about 2 quarts fully ripe strawberries)

1   box **SURE-JELL** Fruit Pectin

½   teaspoon butter or margarine (optional)

7   cups sugar, measured into separate bowl

**BRING** boiling-water canner, half full with water, to simmer. Wash jars and screw bands in hot soapy water; rinse with warm water. Pour boiling water over flat lids in saucepan off the heat. Let stand in hot water until ready to use. Drain well before filling.

**STEM** and crush strawberries thoroughly, 1 layer at a time. Measure exactly 5 cups prepared fruit into 6- or 8-quart saucepot.

**STIR** pectin into prepared fruit in saucepot. Add butter to reduce foaming, if desired. Bring mixture to full rolling boil (a boil that doesn't stop bubbling when stirred) on high heat, stirring constantly. Stir in sugar. Return to full rolling boil and boil exactly 1 minute, stirring constantly. Remove from heat. Skim off any foam with metal spoon.

**LADLE** immediately into prepared jars, filling to within ⅛-inch of tops. Wipe jar rims and threads. Cover with 2-piece lids. Screw bands tightly. Place jars on elevated rack in canner. Lower rack into canner. (Water must cover jars by 1 to 2 inches. Add boiling water, if necessary.) Cover; bring water to gentle boil. Process 10 minutes. Remove jars and place upright on a towel to cool completely. After jars cool, check seals by pressing middles of lids with finger. (If lids spring back, lids are not sealed and refrigeration is necessary.)

*Makes about 8 (1-cup) jars or 128 servings, 1 tablespoon each.*

- - - - - - - - -

*HOW TO MEASURE PRECISELY:* To get exact level cup measures of sugar, spoon sugar into dry metal or plastic measuring cups, then level by scraping excess sugar from top of cup with a straight-edged knife.

# Strawberry-Swirl Cake

Total: 1 hour 35 minutes (includes cooling)

1 package (2-layer size) white cake mix

1 package (4-serving size) **JELL-O** Strawberry Flavor Gelatin

⅔ cup **BREAKSTONE'S** or **KNUDSEN** Sour Cream

⅔ cup powdered sugar

1 tub (8 ounces) **COOL WHIP** Whipped Topping, thawed

1 cup sliced strawberries, plus 2 whole strawberries for garnish

**PREHEAT** oven to 350°F. Grease 2 (8- or 9-inch) round cake pans; set aside. Prepare cake batter as directed on package. Pour half of the batter into medium bowl. Add dry gelatin mix; stir until well blended. Spoon half of the white batter and half of the pink batter, side by side, into each prepared pan. Lightly swirl batters together using a teaspoon. (Do not overswirl, or the color of the cake will be all pink and not pink and white marbled.)

**BAKE** 30 minutes. Cool 30 minutes in pans. Remove to wire racks; cool completely.

**MIX** sour cream and powdered sugar in medium bowl until well blended. Gently stir in whipped topping. Place 1 of the cake layers on serving plate; spread top with 1 cup of the whipped topping mixture. Top with 1 cup of the strawberries and remaining cake layer. Spread top and sides of cake with remaining whipped topping mixture. Garnish with whole strawberries just before serving. Store leftover cake in refrigerator.

*Makes 16 servings, 1 slice each.*

- - - - - - - - - -

*HOW TO PREVENT AIR BUBBLES:* To release any air bubbles from the cake batter, lightly tap cake pans on counter before baking. Any small air bubbles will rise to the surface.

*"Try using other flavors of gelatin to make your own favorite flavor swirl."*
—Sarah Dicello, Kraft Kitchens

# 5 Minute Prep

# NILLA Nibbles

Total: 5 minutes

4   Reduced Fat **NILLA** Wafers

2   tablespoons thawed **COOL WHIP LITE** Whipped Topping

2   medium strawberries, halved

**TOP** each wafer with 1½ teaspoons of the whipped topping and 1 strawberry half.

**SERVE** immediately.

*Makes 1 serving.*

- - - - - - - - -

*SUBSTITUTE:* Prepare as directed, using COOL WHIP FREE Whipped Topping.

## Sensational treats for Healthy Living

 **Mimosa Mold**

Total: 5 hours (includes refrigerating)

1½ cups boiling water

1 package (8-serving size) **JELL-O** Orange Flavor Sugar Free Low Calorie Gelatin

2 cups cold club soda

1 can (11 ounces) mandarin orange segments, drained

1 cup sliced strawberries

STIR boiling water into dry gelatin mix in large bowl at least 2 minutes until completely dissolved. Stir in club soda. Refrigerate 1½ hours or until thickened (spoon drawn through leaves definite impression).

STIR in oranges and strawberries. Pour into 6-cup mold sprayed with cooking spray.

REFRIGERATE 4 hours or until firm. Unmold. Store any leftover gelatin in refrigerator.

*Makes 12 servings.*

CALORIES 15, CARB 3g, TOTAL FAT 0g (0g SAT. FAT), FIBER 0g, PROTEIN 1g

# Very Berry Fruit Cups

Total: 2 hours 15 minutes (includes refrigerating)

¾ cup boiling water

1 package (4-serving size) **JELL-O** Strawberry-Banana Flavor Sugar Free Low Calorie Gelatin

Ice cubes

½ cup cold water

1 cup puréed strawberries

¾ cup thawed **COOL WHIP** Sugar Free Whipped Topping

STIR boiling water into dry gelatin mix in medium bowl at least 2 minutes until completely dissolved. Add enough ice cubes to cold water to measure 1¼ cups. Add to gelatin; stir until slightly thickened. Remove any unmelted ice. Refrigerate 10 minutes or until slightly thickened (consistency of unbeaten egg whites).

ADD strawberries; stir. Pour evenly into 6 dessert dishes.

REFRIGERATE 2 hours or until firm. Store leftover desserts in refrigerator. Dollop each dessert with whipped topping before serving.

*Makes 6 servings.*

CALORIES 90, CARB 19g, TOTAL FAT 1.5g (1g SAT. FAT), LESS THAN 1g FIBER, PROTEIN 1g

## JELL-O Strawberry Mousse Cups

Total: 2 hours 15 minutes (includes refrigerating)

¾  cup boiling water

1  package (4-serving size) **JELL-O** Strawberry Flavor Sugar Free Low Calorie Gelatin

1  cup ice cubes

2  cups thawed **COOL WHIP** Sugar Free Whipped Topping, divided

1  pint strawberries, sliced (about 2 cups), divided

STIR boiling water into dry gelatin mix in large bowl at least 2 minutes until completely dissolved. Add ice cubes; stir until completely melted. Gently stir in 1½ cups each of the whipped topping and strawberries until well blended.

SPOON evenly into 6 small dessert dishes. Refrigerate 2 hours or until firm.

TOP with the remaining ½ cup whipped topping and remaining strawberries just before serving. Store any leftover dessert cups in refrigerator.

*Makes 6 servings, 1 dessert cup each.*

CALORIES 80, CARB 11g, TOTAL FAT 3.5g (1.5g SAT. FAT), FIBER 1g, PROTEIN 1g

## 10 Minute Prep Low-Fat Chocolate-Banana Parfaits

Total: 10 minutes

- 2 cups cold fat free milk
- 1 package (4-serving size) **JELL-O** Chocolate Flavor Fat Free Sugar Free Instant Reduced Calorie Pudding & Pie Filling
- 2 medium bananas, sliced
- ¾ cup thawed **COOL WHIP** Sugar Free Whipped Topping, divided

POUR milk into medium bowl. Add dry pudding mix. Beat with wire whisk 2 minutes or until well blended.

SPOON half of the pudding evenly into 4 dessert glasses. Cover with layers of banana slices, ½ cup of the whipped topping and the remaining pudding. Top with remaining whipped topping.

SERVE immediately. Or cover and refrigerate until ready to serve.

*Makes 4 servings, 1 parfait each.*

CALORIES 160, CARB 33g, TOTAL FAT 2g (2g SAT. FAT), FIBER 3g, PROTEIN 5g

#  Delightful Lemon Mousse with Raspberry Sauce

Total: 4 hours 15 minutes (includes refrigerating)

1½  cups boiling water

1  package (8-serving size) **JELL-O** Lemon Flavor Sugar Free Low Calorie Gelatin

2  teaspoons grated lemon peel

Ice cubes

1  cup cold apple juice

1  tub (8 ounces) **COOL WHIP** Sugar Free Whipped Topping, thawed

1  package (10 ounces) frozen raspberries, thawed, puréed in blender

STIR boiling water into dry gelatin mix and lemon peel in large bowl at least 2 minutes until gelatin is completely dissolved. Add enough ice to apple juice to measure 1¾ cups. Stir into gelatin until slightly thickened. Stir in whipped topping with wire whisk until well blended.

POUR half of the raspberry sauce into 10 dessert dishes. Top with gelatin mixture and remaining raspberry sauce.

REFRIGERATE 4 hours or until firm. Store any leftover dessert in refrigerator. Garnish with fresh raspberries, if desired.

*Makes 10 servings.*

CALORIES 80, CARB 15g, TOTAL FAT 1.5g (1g SAT. FAT), FIBER 2g, PROTEIN 2g

*"This easy and elegant dessert is my favorite way to end a hot summer day."*
*—Sarah Dicello, Kraft Kitchens*

# Angel Lush with Pineapple

Total: 1 hour 15 minutes (includes refrigerating)

1  package (4-serving size) **JELL-O** Vanilla Flavor Instant Pudding & Pie Filling

1  can (20 ounces) **DOLE** Crushed Pineapple in Juice, undrained

1  cup thawed **COOL WHIP** Whipped Topping

1  package (10 ounces) round angel food cake

1  cup fresh mixed berries

MIX dry pudding mix and pineapple with its juice in medium bowl. Gently stir in whipped topping. Let stand 5 minutes until thickened.

CUT cake horizontally into three layers. Place bottom cake layer, cut-side up, on serving plate; top with 1⅓ cups of the pudding mixture. Cover with middle cake layer and additional 1 cup of the remaining pudding mixture. Top with remaining cake layer; spread top with the remaining pudding mixture.

REFRIGERATE at least 1 hour. Top with fresh berries just before serving. Store leftover dessert in refrigerator.

*Makes 10 servings.*

CALORIES 140, CARB 31g, TOTAL FAT 1g (1g SAT. FAT), FIBER 1g, PROTEIN 2g

# Low-Fat Strawberry Shortcut

Total: 15 minutes

1½  quarts (6 cups) strawberries, sliced

¼  cup sugar

1  package (13.6 ounces) fat free pound cake, cut into 12 slices

1  tub (8 ounces) **COOL WHIP** Sugar Free Whipped Topping, thawed

TOSS strawberries with sugar; let stand 10 minutes or until sugar is dissolved.

CUT each slice of pound cake in half horizontally. Place 1 cake piece on each of 12 dessert plates.

SPOON about ¼ cup of the strawberries over each cake piece; top with 2 tablespoons of the whipped topping. Repeat layers. Serve immediately.

*Makes 12 servings.*

CALORIES 170, CARB 36g, TOTAL FAT 1.5g (1g SAT. FAT), FIBER 2g, PROTEIN 2g

**Angel Lush with Pineapple**    88
140 calories, 1g total fat (1g sat. fat), 31g carbohydrate, 1g dietary fiber, 2g protein

**Berry Crunch Parfait**    54
80 calories, 2g total fat (1g sat. fat), 17g carbohydrate, 2g dietary fiber, 1g protein

**Berry Squares**    62
220 calories, 8g total fat (6g sat. fat), 34g carbohydrate, 2g dietary fiber, 3g protein

**Cherry Celebration**    60
120 calories, 3.5g total fat (3.5g sat fat), 22g carbohydrate, 0g dietary fiber, 1g protein

**Citrus Sorbet Pie**    10
300 calories, 9g total fat (5g sat. fat), 49g carbohydrate, 0g dietary fiber, 2g protein

**Classic S'mores**    4
150 calories, 5g total fat (2g sat. fat), 24g carbohydrate, less than 1g dietary fiber, 2g protein

**Creamy Carnival Cups**    38
Strawberry: 160 calories, 6g total fat (3.5g sat. fat), 24g carbohydrate, 0g dietary fiber, 3g protein
*Lemon:* 160 calories, 6g total fat (3.5g sat. fat), 24g carbohydrate, 0g dietary fiber, 3g protein

**Delightful Lemon Mousse with Raspberry Sauce**    86
80 calories, 1.5g total fat (1g sat. fat), 15g carbohydrate, 2g dietary fiber, 2g protein

**Easy Chocolate Éclair Squares**    12
150 calories, 6g total fat (3.5g sat. fat), 23g carbohydrate, less than 1g dietary fiber, 2g protein

**Fast Fruity Delight**    52
160 calories, 3.5g total fat (3.5g sat. fat), 31g carbohydrate, 2g dietary fiber, 2g protein

**Frosty Lemon Ice**    42
10 calories, 0g total fat (0g sat. fat), 1g carbohydrate, 0g dietary fiber, 1g protein

**Frosty Orange Dream Squares**    28
140 calories, 6g total fat (3.5g sat. fat), 21g carbohydrate, 0g dietary fiber, 1g protein

**Frozen Chocolate Soufflés**    32
310 calories, 10g total fat (5g sat. fat), 51g carbohydrate, 1g dietary fiber, 5g protein

**Frozen Coolwich**    48
180 calories, 7g total fat (4g sat. fat), 30g carbohydrate, less than 1g dietary fiber, 2g protein

**Frozen Lemonade Squares**    26
250 calories, 11g total fat (6g sat. fat), 36g carbohydrate, less than 1g dietary fiber, 4g protein

*Very Berry Fruit Cups (page 80)*

**Frozen Peach
Shortcake Squares** 40
220 calories, 10g total fat (7g
sat. fat), 32g carbohydrate, 0g
dietary fiber, 3g protein

**JELL-O Magic Mousse** 64
200 calories, 9g total fat (8g
sat. fat), 30g carbohydrate, 1g
dietary fiber, 2g protein,

**JELL-O Mini Trifle Bites** 18
130 calories, 5g total fat (3.5g
sat. fat), 17g carbohydrate, 0g
dietary fiber, 3g protein

**JELL-O Strawberry
Mousse Cups** 82
80 calories, 3.5g total fat (1.5g
sat. fat), 11g carbohydrate, 1g
dietary fiber, 1g protein

**Key Lime Margarita Pie** 6
310 calories, 15g total fat (10g
sat. fat), 41g carbohydrate, 0g
dietary fiber, 4g protein

**Lemon-Lime Daiquiri
Layered Dessert** 14
260 calories, 12g total fat (8g
sat. fat), 36g carbohydrate, 0g
dietary fiber, 4g protein,

**Low-Fat Chocolate-Banana
Parfaits** 84
160 calories, 2g total fat (2g
sat. fat), 33g carbohydrate, 3g
dietary fiber, 5g protein

**Low-Fat Strawberry Shortcut** 90
170 calories, 1.5g total fat (1g
sat. fat), 36g carbohydrate, 2g
dietary fiber, 2g protein

**Melon Bubbles** 22
15 calories, 0g total fat (0g sat. fat), 2g carbohydrate, 0g dietary fiber, 2g protein

**Mimosa Mold** 78
15 calories, 0g total fat (0g sat. fat), 3g carbohydrate, 0g dietary fiber, 1g protein

**Mixed Berry Freezer Jam** 56
25 calories, 0g total fat (0g sat. fat), 7g carbohydrate, 0g dietary fiber, 0g protein

**Mixed Berry Smoothie:** 46
250 calories, 3g total fat (1.5g sat. fat), 48g carbohydrate, 2g dietary fiber, 9g protein,

**NILLA Nibbles** 76
90 calories, 2g total fat (1g sat. fat), 17g carbohydrate, less than 1g dietary fiber, less than 1g protein

**No-Melt Sundae Pie** 30
280 calories, 14g total fat (9g sat. fat), 37g carbohydrate, less than 1g dietary fiber, 3g protein

**OREO and Fudge Ice Cream Cake** 34
340 calories, 14g total fat (8g sat. fat), 50g carbohydrate, less than 1g dietary fiber, 4g protein

**OREO Ice Cream Shop Pie** 24
320 calories, 12g total fat (6g sat. fat), 50g carbohydrate, 0g dietary fiber, 2g protein

**Peach & Raspberry Trifle** 8
110 calories, 1g total fat (1g sat. fat), 23g carbohydrate, 2g dietary fiber, 3g protein

**PHILADELPHIA "Fruit Smoothie" No-Bake Cheesecake** 58
280 calories, 18g total fat (12g sat. fat), 24g carbohydrate, less than 1g dietary fiber, 6g protein

**Rocket Pops** 44
130 calories, 2.5g total fat (2.5g sat. fat), 26g carbohydrate, 0g dietary fiber, less than 1g protein

**"Sangria" Fruit Cups** 36
150 calories, 2g total fat (1.5g sat. fat) 31g carbohydrate, 1g dietary fiber, 2g protein

**Sparkling Berry Dessert** 66
90 calories, 0g total fat (0g sat. fat), 21g carbohydrate, 0g dietary fiber, 2g protein

**Strawberry Dessert Pizza** 70
340 calories, 18g total fat (10g sat. fat), 41g carbohydrate, less than 1g dietary fiber, 3g protein

**Strawberry-Swirl Cake** 74
240 calories, 8g total fat (4.5g sat. fat), 41g carbohydrate, 0g dietary fiber, 3g protein

*OREO Ice Cream Shop Pie (page 24)*

**Summer Berry Pie** 50
510 calories, 20g total fat (6g sat. fat), 75g carbohydrate, 2g dietary fiber, 3g protein

**SURE-JELL Strawberry Jam** 72
45 calories, 0g total fat (0g sat. fat), 12g carbohydrate, 0g dietary fiber, 0g protein

**Triple Berry Parfaits** 68
150 calories, 3.5g total fat (2.5g sat. fat), 27g carbohydrate, 2g dietary fiber, 4g protein

**Triple-Layer Lemon
Meringue Pie** 20
380 calories, 12g total fat (7g sat. fat), 62g carbohydrate, 0g dietary fiber, 3g protein

**Very Berry Fruit Cups** 80
90 calories, 1.5g total fat (1g sat. fat), 19g carbohydrate, less than 1g dietary fiber, 1g protein

**Wave-Your-Flag Cake** 16
160 calories, 6g total fat (4.5g sat. fat), 25g carbohydrate, 1g dietary fiber, 2g protein

# Index